GHOSTS
OF
DEVIZES

by
John Girvan

Girvan Publications

To Anne, Verity, & Nathan.

Copyright © John Girvan
First Published 1995
by

Girvan Publications
Devizes

ISBN 0 9525953 0 3

British Library Cataloguing in Publication Data
A catalogue record for this book is available from
The British Library

Typeset in 10 point Times Roman
Typeset by Chris Greenwood, Sprint Systems, Devizes
Cover Design and layout, John Girvan
Graphics, Verity Girvan
Printed by Springfords & Rose Ltd.
Devizes, Wilts. England

CONTENTS

Staircase at Devizes Town Hall (Simulacrum)

4

INTRODUCTION

As a local historian and author John Girvan came across numerous references to ghost stories with sightings at buildings in and around Devizes. Among his other subjects John created a talk on ghosts which further developed into a ghost walk around his home town. Not only did people want to hear of ghost stories but also with much curiosity wanted to visit the sites where these instances had occurred.

Over a period of three years, interest in the ghost walk grew when many groups and individuals turned out during the winter months for a walk in the dark. During the walk, recollections are made as to what has been seen, where, and when. You are left to form your own opinion as to how you wish to accept the information, whether you are a devoted believer in ghosts or view it with some scepticism, people like to hear ghostly tales of mystery about the town.

After numerous requests for a book on ghosts this is the culmination of not only existing stories but more recent sightings with related information, witches and wizards have been included with references to the plague that swept through the west country.

By using small fragments of objects the author has had psychometries carried out under controlled conditions with amazing results, whatever you make of the information it produces most uncanny data.

While carrying out research, John came across the arm of George Carpenter who committed a murder in 1812! Interesting new material has come to light with anecdotes and references and so it is through popular demand that this book has been published.

Other books by the author include:
Showmen of Wiltshire; Devizes in Focus
and as co-editor; Devizes in Camera I and II.

MARKET PLACE

The Bear Hotel

Facing onto the Market Place from the south west the Bear Hotel has greeted many a weary traveller, having been a hostelry before 1559. Many famous patrons have used this coaching inn as their stopping off station while passing through the West Country, including King George III accompanied by Queen Charlotte and the notorious Judge Jeffreys who had sent many a man to death by the hangman's noose.

A scratched message has been left on one of the panes of glass in a bedroom window bearing witness that not all travellers enjoyed their journey through Devizes, as the pathetic message reads:-

"John Blome, merchant, on his way from London to Bath and Bristol for execution February 1760."

The ghost of the Grey Lady leaves her presence at what is now the hotel reception area. When she was first seen the Bear Hotel was two separate buildings divided by private apartments. At that time a lady draped in grey was seen passing through the corridor of these apartments before disappearing through the wall. Even though the apartments and corridor are no longer there she has always been seen in this same location.

Other sightings have been made at the Bear Hotel of figures dressed in costumes of an earlier period of time.

The Bear Hotel (Drawing G. A. Renvoize)

6

Ruth Pierce

One of the most famous stories of Devizes is the tale of Ruth Pierce who had told a lie with a fatal consequence. This true story is inscribed on a plaque on the eastern face of the Market Cross which was erected in 1814 by Henry Addington MP for Devizes.

The inscription reads:-

"On Thursday, the 25th January, 1753, Ruth Pierce, of Potterne, in this County, agreed with three other women to buy a sack of wheat in the Market, each paying her due proportion towards the same. One of these women, in collecting the several quotas of money, discovered a deficiency, and demanded of Ruth Pierce the sum which was wanting to make good the amount. Ruth Pierce protested that she had paid her Share, and said; "She wished she might drop down dead if she had not." She rashly repeated this awful wish, when to the consternation and terror of the surrounding multitude, she instantly fell down and expired, having the money concealed in her hand."

The reality of this dramatic event is that Ruth Pierce could well have suffered from a heart attack having told this lie. Her body was placed onto a hurdle used at the market and taken to Parnella House, home of the surgeons John and William Clare. This stone pillared building across the Market Place has a statue of Aesculapius, the Greek God of healing, looking down from a niche in the facade.

After examination, Ruth's body was taken to an outbuilding at the rear of the premises where she was laid out on a stone slab. It is from here that she now haunts as a ghost and has been seen several times in the passageway alongside Parnella House.

The story of Ruth Pierce was originally displayed on a board attached to the Market House, since demolished, as an awful warning. It was replaced by a stone inscription affixed to the twin columned monument supporting a stone black bear. This was removed in 1806 from the centre of the Market Place and the bear was placed on the porch of the Bear Hotel where it is seen today.

The Black Bear
Monument
Demolished
1806
(Waylen Print)

New Market
Cross
Erected 1814
(Waylen Print)

The Little Brittox

Leading off the Market Place, No 4 the Little Brittox was once a fashionable ladies' outfitters. The ghost appears of an elderly lady dressed all in black with a shawl. It is thought to be Mrs Pritchard who owned the shop which bore her name and is now a delicatessen.

Other visions and audible sounds have been experienced in flat apartments above the shops in the Little Brittox, including an alarming incident reported by a young lady who could feel the intimate presence of a man in her bedroom while she was alone.

Public Burnings

What today seems a most barbaric and horrific death was burning people alive which was practised in this area.

Fire was used as a cleansing force to rid heretics of their religious beliefs, at a time of religious turmoil in the 16th Century. This martyrdom was the fete of William Prior of Devizes who professed Lollardry and after signing a recantation of his principles at Salisbury was then burned to death as a heretic in 1507 in this cruel manner.

Again in 1523 John Bent who was a tailor by trade was delivered into the flames at Devizes Market Place and burned at the stake for his "denial of doctrine of transubstantiation". He foolishly questioned the cost of pilgrimages and wasting money on offerings to Saints together with critical comments on the sacrament. A wood carving depicting John Bent being consumed by flames is at Devizes Museum and is thought to have been carved at the time.

A most horrific and graphic account describes the burning of John Maundrell of Rowde, John Spicer and William Coberley who spoke out against the preaching of the Vicar of Keevil. They were first laid in the stocks then taken to the county jail at Fisherton, Salisbury

On an earlier occasion John Maundrell was sentenced to prominade around Devizes Market Place wearing a white sheet carrying a candle in his hand as a penance, but on the fatal day of the 24th March 1556 the three of them were taken to Wilton Road, Salisbury, where two stakes were ready for them. After being stripped down to their shirts Spicer exclaimed "this is the joyfulest day that I ever saw". Soon after lighting the fires, death came rapidly to Maundrell and Spicer, but due to the wind changing direction Coberley's body was only scorched which resulted in his left arm dropping off. He was seen to be leaning forward against his chains with his right hand gently striking his chest and bleeding at the mouth. When those who witnessed the event all thought he was dead he again showed life by lifting himself upright again.

As reported in Fox's Book of Martyrs "they gave their bodies to the fire and their souls to the Lord for testimony of their truth".

Another technique to accelerate death by burning was to hang a bag of gunpowder around the neck of the unfortunate victim.

John Bent burned alive in the Market Place 1523
(Wood carving, Devizes Museum)

THEATRES

Electric Picture Palace

When the Electric Picture Palace as it was known opened in Devizes in 1912 it caused a sensation attracting people from a wide area. As a cinema it proved very popular boasting it's own generated electricity.

After a drastic fire in 1932 it's interior was rebuilt complete with a fully equipped stage. Many theatres in this country have a ghost as does the Palace. It was Mr Bill Bobby on taking over as manager who began to investigate a ghost on the premises when several instances came to light.

In 1975 three gentlemen spent the night in the Palace attempting to contact a ghost. While in an upstairs room they heard footsteps coming towards them, one of the three had a psychic sense and was able to see the figure of a man approaching wearing 18th century costume, neither of the other two could see anything, however one had a camera who, under direction, pointed it to take three photographs. The following morning the film was anxiously developed producing negatives, strangely they would not produce prints, but on inspection one of the three negatives showed an image of a ghost. Unfortunately within the space of a week this image faded away only to leave the three negatives with just a view across the room.

Other sightings of figures have been reported at the Palace including one in the adjoining premises. It is said that Mr Bobby himself has been seen sitting in a certain seat in the cinema since his death.

Oddfellows Hall

Another theatre ghost has been reported in Maryport Street at Oddfellows Hall, billed as The Music Hall with nightly performances of variety, concerts, drama and musicals. The Hall remained popular during the 1930s up to its demise after the war.

Monday Market Street Theatre

During the Autumn of 1994 the author was informed of a haunting figure in a storeroom of a supermarket in Monday Market Street. It seemed unlikely that a new supermarket would have a ghost but still reports were being made by the store assistants. Two sightings were made of a figure of a man all in black wearing a large hat.

Further enquiries were made into the former property which stood on the site, and it was revealed that sightings had also been made at the agricultural engineers, T H White. Yet further research at Devizes Museum eventually turned up two advertisement posters for a theatre in Monday Market Street on this same site. Very little is known of this theatre where it is thought the ghost originated.

As printed in the poster dated 1833 it had boxes, a pit and a gallery with seat prices ranging from 6 pence to 3 shillings. This is a case where a ghost has reappeared in a new building having originated in an earlier one demolished on the same site.

Poster: Monday Market Street Theatre 1833 (Devizes Museum)

THE CASTLE

Queen Matilda

The account of how Queen Matilda, daughter of King Henry, made her escape from Devizes Castle is something of a ghostly story in itself. The year was 1141 when a state of civil war was in progress to establish who should have the throne of England. Matilda was pursued to Devizes from Ludgershall Castle, arriving at Devizes Castle more dead than alive, disguised as a man riding astride a horse. There she was held under seige by Stephen of Bolois who also coveted the throne.

To effect an escape Matilda was wrapped in bandages and placed in a coffin and carried on a litter slung between two horses as a corpse. She was able to escape through the army of Stephen's besieging forces and get safely to Gloucester. In gratitude for help from the people of Devizes she granted the first Borough Charter of 1141 which reads:-

> *"I grant to my Burgesses of Devizes that for their allegiance, they shall be free of land-toll, ferry toll, fair toll and all other customs throughout my land and the seaports. And I will ordain that they and their servants and all their goods shall have my secure peace; and moreover, none shall unjustly disturb them under penalty of ten pounds."*

The Borough was governed by it's Charters until the Municipal Corporation Act of 1835. The castle as seen today was built in Victorian times by Valentine Leach, still accommodating the ghosts from the past.

Borough Coat of Arms
1141-1974, now the Town
Coat of Arms

Queen Matilda (Author's Collection)

Lady Isabella

A ghost story which dates back to the 12th century is that of Lady Isabella who was the daughter of a Norman Lord residing in Devizes Castle, described by chroniclers of that period as being the strongest in Europe.

The name of Isabella was very popular with the Normans who had invaded and overrun this country. Edward II's wife was named Queen Isabella who received the grant of Devizes Castle as part of her dower and Richard II married an Isabella of Valois as his second Queen when she was only 9 years old in 1396.

It was met with disapproval when in Devizes a Lady Isabella was having a relationship with one of the local boys of the town. It was considered a disgrace by the Norman Overlords that this union should continue. She was therefore forbidden to see the boy and was confined within the castle, but the story goes that Isabella would steal away from the security of the stronghold to continue meeting him. When her escapades were discovered her father resorted to locking Isabella in her room. After finding that even this did not stop her he took the drastic measure to brick her up into a basement room to hide the shame she had brought upon her family. It was here that she died entombed.

The site of this room now forms the base of the north tower visible as a circular room without an entrance door or window and it is from here that she haunts. Most ghosts appear in monochrome but Isabella is wearing a dark blue dress. When first seen she appeared as a young girl but when seen recently she appeared to have aged, having a stooping posture, walking with a stick, but still wearing her same dark blue dress.

MARYPORT

Brownston House

Sited under the shadow of St Mary's Church tower is Brownston House, circa 1720. This fine Georgian stone and brick building presents a majestic picture within its perimeter wall.

In one of the back bedroom windows a figure has been seen of a young lady reputed to be Princess Augusta Sophia born 8th November 1768, the sixth child and daughter of George III. She was first seen when the building was used for accommodation for nurses who worked in the nearby hospital. The Princess stayed at the house with General Thomas Garth who was her lover, and held the post of Equerry to the King. She was quite a lady of attention with a spritely manner which caused banter from Mr Turbulent who called her "La coquette corrigee" (flirtatious and flighty).

In 1789 her brother the Duke of York, escorted her to a ball and fought a duel with Colonel Lennox who had made eyes at her. The ball broke up in disarray. The Princess also had a supposed attachment to the Prince Royal of Denmark. It is said she enjoyed her visit to Devizes at Brownston House, so much so, causing her to return as a ghost.

Quakers' Walk

The name Quakers' Walk is a corruption of the name Keepers' Walk which was the entrance to the deer park and Roundway House. An attractive avenue of trees once lined this walk which suffered badly during a storm. It is here that a family group of ghosts are reputed to have been seen donned in Quakers' clothes of grey including high crowned hats for gentlemen, and long dresses worn with bonnets for ladies. A theory is that they visit the Quakers' burial ground at Hillworth Park, with a wrought iron gate bearing the sign "Friends Burial Ground 1665" at the entrance.

An attractive Queen Anne conservatory was once used by Quakers in the centre of the park when bodies were laid in the basement before burial in the cemetery. The gravestones have now been removed from the graves since the park was planted out with ornamental flowerbeds. Records show in 1678 Quakers had also been buried near to the site of the gallows in an area beyond the parish boundaries. Quakers first came to Devizes during the 17th century.

St Mary's Walk and Church

The approach to the walkway alongside St Mary's Church from Commercial Road is by way of stone steps. It is uncertain when these steps were built as they are not shown on Edward Dore's map of 1759 but are shown on the ordnance survey of 1885. Many Devizes people do not like using this walkway at night because of the haunting stories of the burials. Every time that cuttings are dug alongside for building construction, human remains invariably turn up.

During the building of Chantry Court and before that the Regal Cinema and before that Bennett's Antique Store, human remains were found. At the last excavation up to sixteen skeletons were unearthed which were re-interred at the cemetery. The situation dates back to the civil war when numerous bodies had to be buried and the land adjoining the churchyard was conveniently used. However there are a number of bodies still buried beneath the walkway.

With this in mind the children's activity is recalled of "Only stepping on whole paving slabs and never the joints". The old saying goes that "Should there ever be any spirits underneath, they can reach up between the slabs to grab you".

A nice old story is told in Devizes of a mysterious church cat at St Mary's Church. This cat could only be heard "miaowing" but never found, even during the services the cat was heard but exhaustive searches afterwards could not find it. It was later when repairs were being carried out on the church wall that the petrified remains of a cat were found built into the wall. The builders not wishing to build the remains back into the wall, found a space in the graveyard where they buried the cat's remains. Ever since this was done the cat was never heard again.

The White Bear

The White Bear, formerly known as The Talbot, in the ownership of St Mary's Church, stands where the 16th century medieval market place was sited. This drovers' inn was visited by an old lady who wanted to stable her horse while visiting the market. On leading the horse through the front passage it slipped falling into a cellar which was left open. Unfortunately her horse died from the fall which outraged the lady who then disclosed she was a witch. Whereupon she placed a curse on the cellar vowing it would be forever dark, dank and useless. However the landlord, not wishing to be beaten by the witch's curse, subsequently grew mushrooms in the cellar. In recent years mushrooms have been grown in this same cellar where the bones of a horse have also been found.

The Three Crowns

The Three Crowns Public House in Maryport Street presents an attractive roof line with timber framed Jacobean gables. Originally a lodging house and brewery providing their own beer and a special French brandy for their customers.

A blue heritage plaque on the white rendered front of this 17th century building records the first landlord in 1849.

A ghost has been seen in an upstairs room approached through the double doors across the courtyard into the room which now houses the skittle alley. The female spector is clothed in a wedding dress and is known as "The Lady in White" and stands in the location of her bedroom where she sobs, head bowed under a heavy lace veil. This sad figure of a young lady is also known as the "Jilted Bride" as she waits for her partner who did not turn up for the wedding. It is unknown why he failed to turn up for the wedding ceremony, whether he had met with an unfortunate accident or had second thoughts, we may never know, but still she waits for him as the unhappy jilted bride.

The Three Crowns (Author's Collection)

18

Another incident has been reported when the figure of a lady suddenly appeared at the downstairs bar. She was dressed in a long flowing dress but did not move or speak. To the amazement of those who saw her the figure faded away just as mysteriously as she had appeared. Was she the jilted bride? or indeed someone else.

Duck's Newsagents

It marked the end of an era in Devizes when the newsagents moved from the end of Sheep Street, then popularly known as Duck's Corner. The move to No 11 Maryport Street enabled the family to expand the family business in 1958.

One of the first tasks in the premises was to drain the flooded cellar, however the workmen felt an uneasy atmosphere and refused to work alone down there. When the work was completed the remains of a wreath and a broken off shovel were found.

Initially rooms above the shop were used as residence where the shadow of a man has been seen together with a sensation of being touched on the shoulder. One summer evening when returning back to the premises Mrs Duck was alarmed to see smoke bellowing across the road from an upstairs window and heard a voice of a young girl calling. Running into the building she opened the door to this particular room but found nothing, only a very chilled atmosphere.

Later Miss Dee from the adjoining shop recalled a story she had heard dating back to the 1890s when No 11 was a ladies gown shop. At that time the young girl apprentices would live-in above the shop. Unfortunately one day there was a fire when one of the girls was caught in the blaze and died.

This incident that took place in 1890 had now been witnessed in 1958.

A further development arose when the rooms above the shop were converted from private residence into commercial use. On removing the plaster and linings, charred timbers were discovered indicating that there had indeed been a substantial fire in this same room, still to this day retaining an atmosphere of presence.

SOUTHBROOM

Devizes School

Just why Maria Heathcote appears as a ghost at Devizes School is still a mystery. Her portrait hangs in the hall of the school which was part of the original house built in 1773 on the estate where a former house was destroyed by fire. The portrait of Maria Heathcote was painted in 1724 showing her at the time of her marriage when she was eighteen years old. The artist was Van-Der-Bank and was a gift to the school by Sir Humphrey Mynors.

Before the school became comprehensive it was known as Southbroom School taking on the name of the old house. The property descended to Maria who married George Heathcote of London. She died in 1792 and is buried in St John's Church cemetery. The ghost is also referred to as "The Grey Lady" but as she appears in the same clothes as in the painting she is thought to be Maria.

Pupils at the school have carried out extensive research to trace the mystery of their ghost and have come up with several stories. At one time a gardener on the estate was found hanging in a tree and someone had jumped from the roof of the house to commit suicide. Also it was believed that a murder was committed in the attic rooms, and so the mystery of the ghost persists.

However she is kept very much alive by the pupils as the new intake of children start for the first time at the school. They are told of the ghost of Maria in the portrait and instructed to knock on the hall table twice then to walk around it four times when Maria is reputed to appear.

London Road

Beyond Southbroom in the London Road a large house has a strange presence in its basement cellar. Apart from sounds and poltergeist movements the following story was reported. In an effort to improve the level of the cellar floor, a concrete mix was laid. After this was shovelled in and finally smoothed it was left to dry out with the cellar door shut. No one had been down into the cellar but when it was looked at again a set of mysterious footprint impressions were left in the new concrete floor.

Maria Heathcote (Painting, Devizes School)

LONG STREET

The Museum

The Wiltshire Archaeological and Natural History Society moved into Long Street in 1874. By 1902 No 40 Long Street, a former private school for girls, was acquired as a library and archive for the new Museum. It is here that the ghost of Maude Edith Cunnington is reputed to appear. She was the wife of Benjamin, curator of the Museum, and mayor of Devizes in 1912 and 1929. Her grandfather, Valentine Leach, was responsible for the rebuilding of Devizes Castle.

Seated at a large wooden table in the library Mrs Cunnington's spector has been seen reading through old ledgers. At one time a girl student worked part time at the Museum where her duties included announcing to visitors that "the Museum will close in five minutes time". She reported to the curator with some concern that an elderly lady in the library took no heed to her announcements, only to be told that she'd been asking the ghost in residence to leave.

Maude Edith
Cunnington   (Devizes Museum)

Other sightings and sounds had been heard by two sisters who were cleaners at the Museum, after closing time when they were the only people in the building. One of these ladies engaged in a conversation with who she thought was her sister in the adjoining room, only to discover it was Mrs Cunnington, as her sister had earlier gone downstairs.

On repeated occasions while they were both on the ground floor, footsteps and the movement of a chair could be heard in the library above.

Mrs Cunnington was a noted archaeologist who conducted the excavations at All Cannings Cross. She died in 1951 at the age of 81.

Antique Shop

An antique shop at No 50 Long Street is yet another timber framed commercial property where a ghost has been reported. Appearing as an old woman at the rear of the shop, after extensive building alterations to remove later partition walls exposing the original timbers. A fragment of gravestone was found in the cellar at this time which is in close proximity to St John's churchyard at the rear. Original parchment deeds to the property still survive dating back to the 17th century.

The Elm Tree

The infamous Captain Jones in 1643 had been using the Elm Tree, formerly known as the Salutation, as a base while in Devizes. As a Royalist supporter of the King during this period of civil war, he commanded a contingent of cavalier soldiers with two hundred horses. There were also a number of Roundhead soldiers he held captive at the rear of the inn.

On hearing that Sir William Waller was approaching from Calne, Jones took his men to engage battle with these parliamentarians. Unfortunately his soldiers were overpowered causing Jones to break away returning to the inn where, unknown to him, the Roundhead captives had become free and were waiting for him. As he approached the entrance Captain Jones was shot in the head outside the inn where the night before he was insisting that everyone should drink the King's health with "strong waters and wines".

The ghost of Captain Jones is said to return to the inn to drink again a toast to the King.

Death of Captain Jones 1643 (Waylen Print)

The Town Hall

Just across the road from the Elm Tree is the Town Hall where the ghost of a cavalier is also said to haunt, but it is thought to be one of the same person, as Captain Jones was brutally killed close by. Staff at the Town Hall can sense his presence and he has been seen descending the winding staircase.

On one occasion the caretaker's dog stood at the bottom of the stairs and was attracted to something halfway up the staircase. Although nothing was visible to the human eye the dog was reacting strangely to something it could apparently see.

Another ghost of a cavalier manifests at Devizes Castle donned with plumed hat, leather boots and tunic, could this be Captain Jones yet again? or another unidentified cavalier.

ST JOHN'S STREET

Old Butcher's Shop

Many Devizes people recall the story of the unfortunate fate of the butcher who traded at his shop in St John's Street, now converted into a residential house. At the time someone had cause to call on the butcher who lived alone. After repeated knocking at the front door they were unable to make him hear. With the knowledge that he should be on the premises they decided that the only option was to force the front door to gain entry, concerned as to the man's well-being.

After searching the three floors he could not be found. Carcasses of meat for the shop were stored in the cellar as this would have been the coolest place. It was there that they found the butcher hanging on one of his meat hooks amongst the other carcasses. Very few other details are known of the incident and it was presumed that he had committed suicide.

St John's Street, No 29/30

An adjoining corridor in the top floor of No 29/30 St John's Street is the location of a ghost sighting. In earlier times these two properties were in the single ownership of one family. The figure of a lady has been seen on several occasions walking along this corridor when she would turn at one particular spot to walk through the wall. It was later discovered that at this very spot in the wall is where an original doorway used to be sited, but was removed and blanked off. This room was known for many years as the Ghost Room.

Old Lock-Up

Set into the wall at the back of the Town Hall is the sturdy metal entrance door to the old lock-up. It is said to be haunted, but very little information is known of a ghost. This basement cell must have been very forbidding when used for confinement giving rise to a ghostly presence within.

St John's Alley

Entering the cobbled St John's Alley is like stepping into the past with its mid 16th century timber overhanging building forming a pair of two storey commercial shops, with an earlier three storey timber framed merchant's house beyond.

As a member of the Trust for Devizes the author was present when the following incident happened. When the building was derelict prior to its restoration as seen today it was open to the public on certain weekends. On such an occasion the author was in a ground floor room providing historical information to visitors. The room was empty apart from a large stone fireplace, so it was strange when a teenage girl entered the room taking care to walk around keeping close to the walls.

On enquiring as to why she took this course the girl realized that the large table she was walking around was only visible to her. She then explained she could also see a high backed chair in the corner of the room and an elderly lady dressed in black with her head covered sitting over by the fireplace.

Later in the afternoon a middle aged lady walked around the room in the same manner. Amazed to have witnessed this for a second time the author asked if she was avoiding the table. The lady was surprised when he described the scene to her as she thought that only she could see the elderly lady and the furniture in the room.

After the author had explained that it was actually a young girl who had seen this earlier, the woman exclaimed that it must have been her daughter who had inherited her ability of second sight.

Neither the mother nor the daughter knew they had both visited the building. Although the author had been present he had seen nothing.

Dowsing rods have successfully been used to pick up activity when near the large stone fireplace. During the restoration of the building two names were found scratched onto a window pane, that of "Elisa Bryant and J J Bryant, Woodbro, Sept 8th 1832". A member of the Phoenix Group was consulted to psychometrise the piece of glass without prior knowledge of its origin. A man and lady were visually described, among the references, the lady appeared to link with the sighting, wearing long black clothes with a hooded bonnet. She was very weak, frail and in pain and was seen by the psychometrist to be sitting in a chair.

The image of the building manifested through hand contact with the glass as long, dark and narrow, decorated as black and white with small paned windows overlooking cobblestones. This description reflects St John's Alley which was unknown at the time of the pychometry.

St. John's Alley (Drawing G. A. Renvoize)

ESTCOURT HILL

Sexton's Cottage

The best view of the Sexton's Cottage is from the south east corner of St John's churchyard. This stone building formerly an alms house and in later years the residence of the Sexton of St John's Church was built in 1615.

A ghost has been sighted here on several occasions described as a young lady dressed in a bonnet and cloak. She is seen through the leaded glass windows carrying a candle. In the flickering candlelight she passes across, first the upper bedroom windows then the windows on the ground floor. At the time the house was unoccupied, the figure was described as looking like a nurse doing a night time round checking the rooms. An interesting link with this sighting was discovered on Dore's illustrated map of Devizes dated 1759 where the building is referred to as St John's Hospital.

The present occupants of the cottage state they have never visually seen the ghost but describe the building as having a kind and caring atmosphere with a sense of presence.

Sexton's Cottage (Drawing J. Girvan)

Railway Tunnel

What to do with a redundant railway tunnel was resolved in 1983 when an idea was mooted for a firing range, and so the Wiltshire Shooting Centre was formed. The structure was ideal for such a use as it was subterranean, but ever since it was taken over a poltergeist has been experienced with a whole catalogue of happenings reported, from ledgers moving out of a cabinet, cups, pennies, clays and numerous other objects have come flying through the air of their own accord.

After the premises have been shut for the night the noise of a pickaxe has been heard chipping away, this was the technique used when the tunnel was first built in 1861 by navvies using handtools, barrows and carts.

The tunnel was constructed as a cutting with retaining walls at each side then arched over and backfilled with earth. It follows the curve of Devizes Castle moat above. Originally the moat was 30-40 feet deep rather than the 16 feet of today. A local newspaper dated 23rd January 1862 reported a human skeleton was found in the tunnel cutting, 6 feet below the present depth of the moat. It was lying on its back with its head pointing north west.

A lady visiting the range in 1991 was mediumistic and was able to detect a strong presence at several points within the tunnel. Shadow figures have been seen in the "step-ins", these are alcoves let into the walls of the tunnel.

While work was being carried out by builders to extend the range facilities the level of poltergeist action increased when it was thought that the alterations were causing a disturbance. Knocking could be heard within an empty locked room. On another occasion after the range had been shut down for the night and security sensors switched on, as the outer door was being locked a violent shaking was heard from inside the inner door. There was no explanation for this. Since the builders have left the site things have now settled down.

Entrance into the Wiltshire Shooting Centre is by way of Station Hill from the Market Place, through the car park which was constructed on the site of the original Great Western Railway Station, opened in 1857.

The Sarcophagus

A curious sarcophagus tomb is found in the far corner of St John's churchyard known by many as the "tea-caddy tomb". Unusually shaped with a top larger than its base it has given rise to curious stories. Children have been placing small stones on the upper projecting lip of the stone tomb when it is said that the stones will move! But you are unable to watch them, as after the stones have been placed, you have to move away, and then return to see they have changed position. This same story was repeated by an elderly gentleman while on the Ghost Walk, who, as a child also used to do this.

Another phenomenon of the tomb gives rise to the expression "the whispering tomb". After a heavy rainstorm, water seeps into a lower compartment below the ground which produces a gurgling sound, some time later sounding quite eerie. Unfortunately there does not appear to be any historical data relating to this unusual tomb.

Another amazing tale, if somewhat improbable, is of a secret passageway leading to the castle from a tomb in this churchyard.

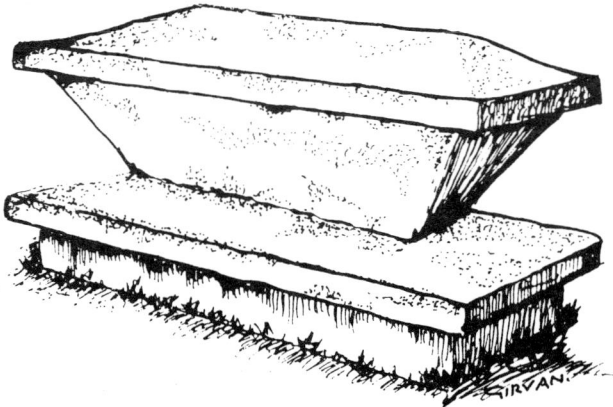

The Sarcophagus, St. John's Churchyard
(Drawing J. Girvan)

The Gallows

One of the oldest footpaths in the town ascends Estcourt Hill from the railway footbridge via St John's churchyard, which was the route from the Castle to an area of grass once the site of the old town gallows. It was here in the 12th century that executions by hanging were carried out by the Normans who had built Devizes Castle. A hanging in those times involved suspending the unfortunate victim by the neck with a noose over a simple crossbar. Death was caused by asphyxiation, rather than the dislocation of the vertebrae by the drop method of hanging. Therefore it could be a long and lingering death by choking. What often happened after hoisting up the condemned person was that relatives would hang onto the legs to speed up the process bringing a more rapid death.

On this site a ghost appears as a grey figure of a man with a featureless face who hangs by a rope around his neck while the end of the rope ascends up into the sky into infinity. He appears to gently swing to and fro with his feet just off the ground, this sighting has been seen by several people at different times.

While on the Ghost Walk at the site of the Gallows, dowsing rods were used by members of the Phoenix Spiritual Development Group from Calne with interesting results. They were able to locate two parallel lay-lines transversing the site on a diagonal plane. By using the rods, a high energy force was located towards the north side of the enclosure. A suggestion was made that this located spot could well have been the original entrance to the Gallows as it was also in alignment with the Castle across the valley, and the nearest point to the end of the pathway along which the condemned person would have been led to the site. This energy force led towards the centre of the enclosure where it abruptly stopped which could be linked to the scene of the execution when the victim's life was terminated.

Indeed numerous people while on the Walk have experienced a cold spot at the centre when a drop in temperature is associated with a presence. There have been several walkers who, being of a sensitive nature, were unable to enter the enclosure having a feeling that the site radiated an uneasy atmosphere, including a physical experience of illness.

Scene of an execution recreated for an amateur documentary film in 1976 near to the site of the old gallows on Estcourt Hill. (Photographed by the Author).

On Edward Dore's map of Devizes dated 1759 the gallows site is shown as a pond at the end of the road marked as Gallows Ditch, which formed a defensive dyke around the castle inner bailey. The Pond has long since been filled in and is owned by the Town Council, who at one time tried without success to create an ornamental garden on this spot. Estcourt Hill is named Eastcroft Hill on the map (facing page).

There was another site used for hanging in Devizes at the edge of the woods alongside Waiblingen Way. This area was known as "the hangings" where an outcrop of sandstone forms a drop towards the fields, over the years these woods were always considered to have been haunted.

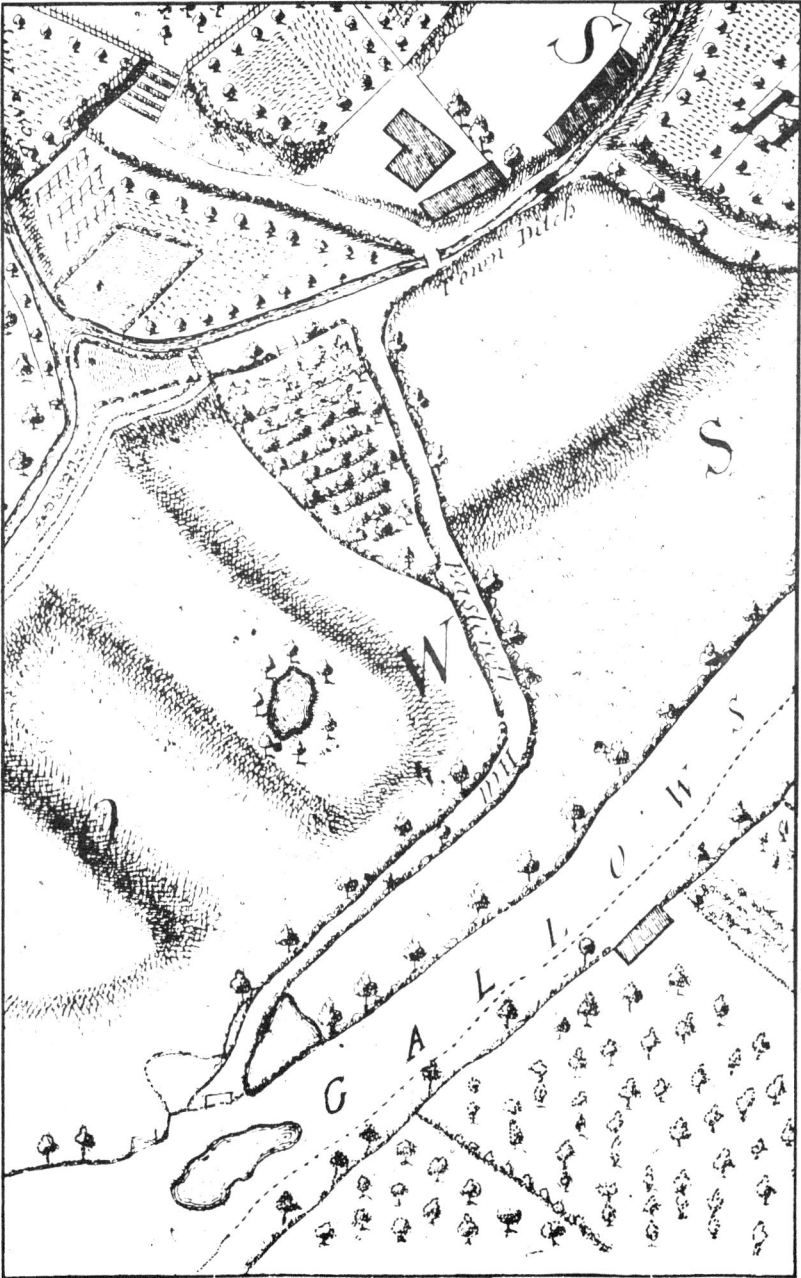

NORTHGATE STREET

Canal Forge

Certain buildings are reputed to have a presence as does the Canal Forge at the Lower Wharf. When the author first acquired the building a loose block of stone was apparent in the solid rear wall. On removing this stone a tiny wooden crucifix was found causing the stone to project. This curious find was shown to a psychic medium who came to visit the forge. On seeing the crucifix and it's location it was explained that it was in fact protecting the building and it was advisable not to remove it.

The medium was able to feel the presence of several people within the forge who, because of the crucifix, were of a peaceful nature, and should the cross be removed it could cause an adverse disturbance.

By using dowsing rods an energy source can be detected around the wall and hearth. Traditionally the Smithy's forge was shrouded with mystery relating back to the Romano-British God, Vulcan.

Canal Forge (Drawing G A Renvoize)

Antique Shop

An antique shop at No 10 Northgate Street is a timber framed commercial premises dated 1640. In later years it was used as a counting house serving Waylens Mill at the rear of the building. The internal timber frame is now exposed, after the fittings and linings were removed during the conversion from a butcher's shop. Following this work, an audible ghost is heard walking up the stairs and across the landing on the first floor.

Old Newspaper Office

When the Wiltshire Times used No 55 Northgate Street as a newspaper office with a resident reporter living in accommodation above the shop, it was clear that a presence was within the building. This 17th century timber framed building forms a semi-detached commercial property clad with hanging tiles on its frontage.

In an outbuilding at the rear of the property burned bones were found in the fire grate of a boiler house which proved to be the remains of babies. Apparently women had been using the building as a base for prostitution at one time and by the evidence of the bones it appeared that unwanted babies had been disposed of in the boiler house giving rise to an uneasy presence. However after the bones were removed, over the years the atmosphere within the building has calmed.

The Nursery

The entrance into Waiblingen Way from Northgate Street is the site of the old Nursery which comprised of a complex of small town houses, most of which had an enclosed narrow winding staircase to the upstairs room which was the location of the sighting of a ghost, appearing as a lady who was seen to sit on the stairs.

She is known to have had an unhappy life with two young sons tragically dying and a husband who did not return from the war, leaving her to die from a broken heart.

This story was related by two ladies who lived in the same house as young children with their parents. Their memories of this figure still remain with them today, only to result in a fear of staircases.

The girls' mother remembers how, after putting them as babies to sleep in their cots, they appeared to have been moved into different locations in the room. Due to their tender age they could not possibly have done this themselves.

When the new flats were built, the old Nursery area was raised to the ground but the ghost has reappeared in the new building more or less in the same location as the staircase in the old house.

An elderly man who lived in the new flats could also see the ghost of the lady who he described as sitting in a hole in the wall. Rather than be afraid of her, he used to talk to her as a friendly companion in his flat.

BATH ROAD

Sussex House

Sussex House on the Bath Road backs onto the old Sussex Wharf on the Kennet and Avon Canal. It was during the time when the present new owners were refurbishing the property that sounds were heard of children running across the floor in the top room in 1991. A distinct presence was experienced particularly in this room.

Later as the work progressed the sighting of a little girl in a pretty dress was seen peering around a cabinet in the centre of the room which was formerly the upper servants' quarters. Sussex House was built in 1876 and subsequent enquiries have revealed that the original occupant of the house had two infant deaths within the family, explaining why more than one child had been heard. The scurrying around of children's feet seems to indicate that they are youngsters at play.

Another strange thing has occurred when an infra-red security alarm system was fitted in the building, the alarm would be set off by someone or something activating it in this room. After checks revealed no faults in the system, it was advised that a different type of security alarm should be used working on a different principal.

On another occasion a little girl was seen waving from the window at the rear of the building by a person who immediately thought the child was a visitor in the house. After further enquiries it was revealed that no children had been there at the time.

Braeside House

The present house at Braeside was built in 1913, once the home of the Antarctic explorer, Ernest Shackleton, whose sled, used during his travels, hung in the hall, but unfortunately is now missing. During the first World War the house was used as a Military Hospital and later as additional premises for Devizes Grammar School across the road. Today it is used as an education and conference centre by Wiltshire County Council.

Two lanes run either side of this estate with a wood banding the escarpment as it runs into fields at the rear. A ghost of a girl is reputed to haunt this wood, she is thought to have been murdered while she was a housemaid serving in the former house which occupied the Braeside estate. Little more is known of the ghost but it was an effective deterrent for the Grammar School pupils as the woods were out of bounds at the time.

Shane's Castle

Stories of ghosts and sightings at Shane's Castle over the years have been associated with this castellated toll-house at the fork of the Bath and Chippenham roads entering Devizes, at a time when road traffic was considerably less with the horse and cart outnumbering the motor vehicle.

There is a tale of how a man was killed by a bolting horse outside the building which has given rise to the story that he was the gate-keeper who now appears as a ghost.

A gentleman who lived alone in Shane's Castle has said how he had heard the tollgate creaking as it was opened and closed during the night, long after the gates had been removed.

A mysterious figure has been seen on the roof who was also thought to be the ghost of this gatekeeper.

Shane's Castle was built as a toll-house or turnpike in 1840 to replace the Rowde Gate at the bottom of Dunkirk Hill, formerly known as Rowde Hill. The original entrance door is no longer in use due to its dangerous access onto the very busy roadway. Entry today is by way of a new doorway set at the corner of the building.

Shane's Castle Toll-gate (Devizes Museum)

INSTITUTIONS

The Prison

Devizes Prison was known as the County House of Correction, built in 1810, in an unusual design of a "panopticon". Sited to the west of Devizes it was used for convicts up to the 1914 war, when it housed army detention prisoners. By 1920 it had fallen into disuse when it was bought by W E Chivers of Devizes.

After the executions were carried out at this prison it was always thought to be haunted. At the first execution in 1824 Edward Amor and John Goodman were hanged together on a gallows erected at the gates, and it was reported that twenty thousand people turned out to watch the gruesome spectacle which was illustrated as a line drawing on a broadsheet which served as a programme of the event.

AN ACCOUNT OF THE TRIAL, BEHAVIOUR, AND EXECUTION OF

Edw. Amor, & John Goodman,
WHO SUFFERED THE AWFUL SENTENCE OF THE LAW ON THE
NEW DROP, AT THE PENITENTIARY, DEVIZES,
On Tuesday, the 20th of April, 1824,
FOR THE ROBBERY, AND ATTEMPTED
MURDER OF MR. THOMAS ALEXANDER, OF SOUTH FARM, NEAR ALLCANNINGS, WILTS.

A public hanging was intended to act as a deterrent, but became a popular event attracting large crowds. After the last public hanging at Devizes in 1860 interest had to be quelled and subsequent executions carried out on a gallows built within the prison walls, in an area between the outer cells and the 19 foot high perimeter wall. After an execution the hanged convict was denied a Christian burial and was placed in a pit of lime within the wall in unhallowed ground. The only memorial to their grave was an inscription on a stone slab let into the prison wall.

When the prison was eventually demolished and houses were proposed to be built on the site, an official was instructed to exhume the bodies of the hanged convicts. All that remained of the ten bodies which were dug up from the site, were returned to London in a small envelope which revealed what effect the lime had on the corpses.

However, ever since the remains were exhumed from the site there have been no other recent reports of ghosts, to the relief of the occupants living in the houses there.

Sam Mollart who owned the scrapyard alongside the prison site was convinced it was haunted and would never visit the yard after dark. Most of the metal fittings from the prison after demolition went to the adjoining scrapyard. The engraved memorial stone slabs are said to be used in an ornamental patio having now been turned over face down.

Prison Cell Door

One of the most interesting objects to have survived from the prison is an original cell door complete with its fittings, a squint window, large bolt and hasp. This door is said to emit a presence which has been experienced by several people who have been in contact with it.

Interesting convicts' names have been carved into the inner face of the door, including Peter White, G Willis and I Walker, also a set of circles have been inscribed by using a cutlery fork.

Two psychometries have been carried out on a small piece of wood from this door. Amazing results were received by a postal psychometry from a psychic medium, which revealed a pre-railway era, railings and gate. Also an epidemic and bowls of liquid, which related to the staple diet which was gruel. The date 1913 was identified (the prison closed for convicts prior to the 1914 war). Altogether seventeen references matched researched information. This is only a small extract from the full report.

Members of the local Phoenix Spiritual Development Group produced further psychometry readings, when people crying and calling out were heard, together with the feeling of containment against one's will. The sound of a bell and a continuous creaking sound was heard, cross-referring to the execution death bell and the sound of a treadwheel creaking in motion, installed in 1823. Many other images including a ship at sea (transportation to the colonies) and a long table where meetings on life and death decisions were made. All this information was extracted by psychometry without any prior details whatsoever on the small piece of wood fragment!

Four photographic negative plates were found on the site of the prison, clearly showing the pictures of a man and a young boy on two of them with their convicts numbers shown on the wall over their right shoulder. Psychometries revealed the poverty, hardship and hard times of this period in vivid detail.

Convict No. 403, Devizes Prison
(Author's Collection)

The Workhouse

In 1993 St James' Hospital was demolished, this was the demise of the former Devizes Union Workhouse, originally built in 1836, when 132 paupers were recorded by the Master of the Workhouse in his report.

The design of the building was typical of the period with its geometric square layout and central tower block. This replaced several other buildings that were used in the town for the relief of the poor and needy, providing very basic needs with food, a bath, clean clothes and a roof over their heads.

By 1948 at the start of the National Health Service changes were made as more money became available. The expression inmates was changed to patients, as by this time it had become a home for the elderly and the name changed to St James' Hospital.

There have been numerous sightings of a ghost in this building by nurses and patients. A description of a young girl in a long shapeless dress floating from room to room appearing as a grey translucent figure. She has been seen moving chairs in the dining room and rearranging cutlery on the table. A nurse reported that on several occasions when an elderly patient was close to death, after being placed in a room on their own for peace and quiet, they had been heard talking. When enquiries were made as to who they were in conversation with, the description was always the same, of a young girl in a long flowing dress, and it was thought that this ghost visited them on their death bed.

One explanation of a ghost's appearance is when a building has been structurally altered, it causes a disturbance for the ghost who then comes back to investigate the change. St James' Hospital had gone through this transitional change from the old Workhouse.

It is thought that the ghost was originally a young girl who had tragically died while she was an inmate of the original Workhouse.

The question arises at the time of writing, now that St James' Hospital has been demolished, will the ghost of the girl reappear when a new building is erected on this site?

Plan of
Devizes Union
Workhouse

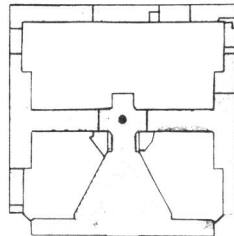

ROUNDWAY HILL

Overlooking Devizes the rolling hills of Roundway Down have long witnessed events of this historic region. As recently as 1995 a lady while out walking her dogs on the south facing chalk slope of Leipzig Plantation, was drawn to a clearing by her dogs barking excitedly at something which had attracted them. After vain attempts at calling them to heel their owner was startled to find them barking at the figure of a girl standing in long coarse grass. The first noticeable thing about her was the very basic and primitive nature of her loose fitting dress made of sack cloth with long sleeves. Her auburn hair parted in the centre, fell over her left shoulder as a single braided plait. This very clear vision of the girl from an earlier period in time, was a positive sighting as she was obviously visible to the dogs who had first found her on this bright sunny morning at 11.30am.

After several minutes of the face to face confrontation the dogs began to settle down as the figure stood motionless. As mysteriously as she had manifested she slowly began to fade until she was no longer visible.

Within a short distance across the valley is the site of Oliver's Castle or Camp. The description of the girl was very similar to that of a person who would have occupied this hill fort, dressed in typical clothes of the iron age period.

Drawing from an
Original sketch
1995
(Drawing J Girvan)

42

The Battle

On the 13th July 1643 the bloodiest battle was fought between the Royalists who occupied Devizes Castle and the Roundhead Parliamentarian Forces under the command of William Waller. A running pursuit by the Royalist Cavaliers chased Cromwell's army across the Downs where they were trapped against the steep slopes of Roundway Hill. Some 800 soldiers on horseback lost their lives when they tumbled down into the valley below. The ditch running from Mother Anthony's Well is said to have ran red with blood giving rise to a ghostly vision of the massacre. This wooded area around the stream can be very eerie as it was reported that the defeated dead soldiers have been seen marching through the heavy mist that often shrouds this site.

Hitch Hiker

During a late night journey to Devizes one winter's evening, a man who was driving his car alone, caught the sight of a girl in a long white dress and windswept blond hair in the beam of his headlights. This ghostly spectre stood at the roadside as if she was beckoning a lift. He was somewhat frightened and decided under the circumstances that he would not stop the car. As the man got closer to Devizes he concluded that he had done the right thing to carry on his journey, when he was aware of a presence in the car. He looked across to the passenger seat and was startled to see her sitting beside him, but by the time he reached the town she had mysteriously disappeared.

Taxi Encounter

In 1994 a taxi driver answering a late call-out from Devizes to Potterne, was alarmed when driving through Potterne woods. A glowing white figure stepped in front of his taxi and unable to stop in time, he appeared to drive straight through the figure. Nothing was visible in either of the rear view mirrors and the driver felt no sensation of an impact. There have been other reported similar sightings in this same area.

THE BLACK DEATH

Ring-a-ring o' Roses, a pocket full of posies
A-Tishoo, A-Tishoo, we all fall down.

This very popular children's nursery rhyme has been recited and taught to very young children since early times but many parents are unaware of the sinister origins of this rhyme which children also enjoy as a ring dance from a tender age. The following lines explain how the rhyme refers directly to the plague known as the Black Death.

Ring-a-ring o' Roses:- refers to the skin blemish appearing as a rosy rash and in an advanced state as red bursting boil sores.

A pocket full of posies:- refers to the garlands of herbs carried in the pockets in a desperate attempt to keep the disease at bay.

A-Tishoo, A-Tishoo:- refers to the final symptom of sneezing often followed with vomiting of blood.

We all fall down:- refers to the fatal consequence of this dreadful plague.

When children play Ring-a-ring o' Roses they invariably do not realise they are re-enacting death when they "all fall down".

This Bubonic Plague was originally known as the Black Death which first appeared in this country in 1333 having come from the far east by way of the docks and ports throughout Britain. The Plague was carried inland by flea-invested rats that were prevalent at a time when hygiene was absent. It was imagined that the "Ghost of Death", in a hooded black shroud would call when you developed the plague.

The Ghost of Black Death (Drawing J Girvan)

44

Over a period of 300 years the Black Death would reappear particularly in the hot summer months up to 1665 when it was known as the Great Plague which gripped the capital city of London with over a third of its population having perished.

Hundreds of people fled London to the countryside to escape the disease. When a member of the household contracted the plague the house was marked with a red cross and the family shut in, the door was only opened to collect the food that was left for them outside. The familiar sound of a man ringing a bell while pushing a handcart sounding the cry "bring out your dead" after which his cart load of dead bodies was taken to the outskirts of the town or village where mass pits were dug. It was the Great Fire of London that brought a halt to this widespread plague as many of the houses of that time were built of timber and thatch. The Fire wiped out not only the insanitary buildings but also the rats with their fleas.

In 1388 conditions were so appalling that King Richard II made a proclamation that "piles of human dung and filth were causing atrocious diseases that it should be cast away the distance of an arrow shot". Cesspools were swarming with rat infestation.

A letter was written in 1607 by the MP for Calne John Noyes from London to his wife warning her not to venture near Devizes. Reports in the Annals of Devizes read that "The Plague broke out again with renewed energy in the summer of 1644, many die daily of it in the Devizes in Wiltshire".

In 1956 workman laying a pipeline on the outskirts of Devizes accidentally came across a pit burial that dated to the Plague. Numerous bones of skeletons were found having been haphazardly buried in the ground typical of the mass graves.

Two independent psychometry tests have been sought by the author on a small piece of bone from this grave. Several members of the Phoenix Group from Calne experienced this traumatic period of the Plague when fear, sickness, nausea and a physical feeling of giddiness could be felt radiating from the fragment.

The explanation of how a psychometry is performed is that material objects are impregnated with events that they have been in contact with from the past. A psychometrist is able to release a semi-conscious physic vision entrapped within the object to produce a mental picture or a sound when in physical contact.

A feeling of poverty, people running in panic to seek a refuge, the piercing eyes of a man in skeletal form shaking with an illness amid an obnoxious smell, was experienced. An interesting sound was heard by a psychic medium on another test. On this occasion a bell was heard described as "not ringing but a dull tolling, not a happy bell".

Another experience included "the feeling of darkness, coldness and death, a man of the cloth, black gown, cross, men, women and children, very dirty, no shoes on their feet, poor people, screams and lots of noise". This reflects in graphic detail this period of 1665 when whole families could die of the Plague. The bodies were buried in mass pits on the outskirts of the town where these bones have been found.

Skeleton Remains from the Plague
(Photo J Girvan)

HANGED MAN'S HAND

It is thought that to possess the severed hand of a man who was hanged for murder would bring mysterious powers to it's owner. There are several of these macabre relics in collections including one in Wiltshire. By repeating the following chant together with keeping the hand with you, it is claimed that a person can carry out a robbery without getting caught.

"Open lock to the dead man's knock,
Fly bolt and bar and band
Nor move nor swerve, joint muscle or nerve
To the spell of the dead man's hand.
Sleep all who sleep, wake all who wake
But be as dead, for the dead man's sake
To the spell of the dead man's hand."

A highwayman was often known to carry a severed hand, usually having removed it from a corpse on a gibbet which was sited at a crossroads on the old coach roads. Even bodies have been known to have a hand removed while in a mortuary prior to burial. Another chant relates to a hand known as the Hand of Glory.

"Let those who rest, more deeply sleep
Let those awake, their vigils keep
Oh Hand of Glory, shed thy light
Direct us to our spoils tonight."

In a Wiltshire village a man was known to have carried out a series of robberies but there was no evidence to prove this and he was never apprehended. When the old gentleman died and subsequent new owners bought the house some years later, it was decided to re-thatch the old cottage. On removing the thatch a severed hand was found in the straw just above the window of the old man's original bedroom. The hand had been dipped in pitch to preserve it.

A method used to embalm a severed hand is that it should be first drained of blood and then soaked in a solution of saltpetre, salt and pepper then dried in the sun for two weeks.

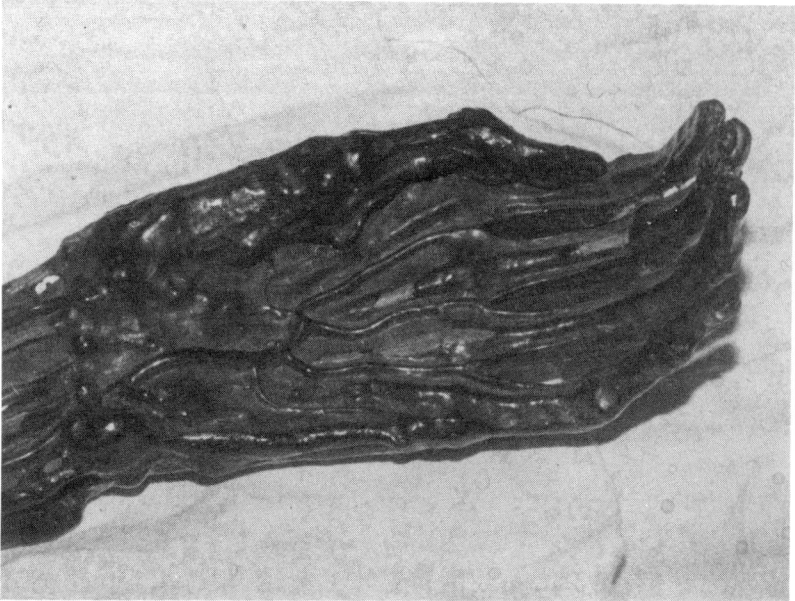

Severed Hanged Man's Hand (Photo J Girvan)

A Severed Hand

Another case of a hanged man's hand being severed from a corpse of a murderer is that of a young Spaniard named Serafin Manzano. His execution on 11th April 1860 at Devizes Prison marked the last public hanging at the prison. The event was not to be missed as a crowd of 13,000 had gathered to watch the spectacle on a scaffold erected at the front gates. Manzano had been convicted for the brutal murder of Anastasia Trowbridge, wife of a road worker at Tollard Royal.

Executioner Calcraft had arrived to carry out his duties to hang the Spaniard who was very repentant of this atrocious murder which left his victim hacked by a razor with apparent saw cuts inflicted after death.

But on the morning of the day of execution the Governor, Mr Alexander, was approached by a gentleman from Frome with a request for the amputated hand from the corpse of Serafin Manzano. It was not uncommon for bodies of murder criminals to be used for medical surgeons' practise. After permission from Mr H N Goddard, the High Sheriff of Wiltshire, the severed hand was given to the man who believed it would assist the healing of an open sore on his neck.

Hanged Man's Arm

Of all the strangest things to be found during a house clearance must be the left arm of George Carpenter. On the 28th December 1812, two young men, George Ruddock aged 20 and George Carpenter aged 21 went to Roddenbury Farm near Longleat where they murdered Mr Webb, a farmer and his maid servant. The motive for the murder is unknown.

They were tried at the County Court at Salisbury where they were both sentenced to death for the double murder. From there they were taken to Warminster where a gallows had been erected on the Downs above the town.

On the 15th March 1813 the execution was carried out, this was thought to be the last public hanging in Wiltshire when a cart was used. Subsequent hanging methods were carried out using the trap door drop method. After the pair had been pinioned and nooses drawn around their necks, George Ruddock jumped from the cart causing an instantaneous death, but his companion in a desperate panic, held onto the cart which impaired his fall, causing an agonizingly painful death. The bodies were then taken down and returned to Salisbury where a surgeon dissected them.

It is not known why George Carpenter's arm was saved. It is still perfectly preserved with its flesh and skin from the shoulder to the hand, though weighing considerably less in a dried state. Varnishing has turned it dark brown in colour. The arm was formerly in the possession of a local surgeon who kept it in a wooden box and has recently been seen by the author in this state at the Police Headquarters in Devizes.

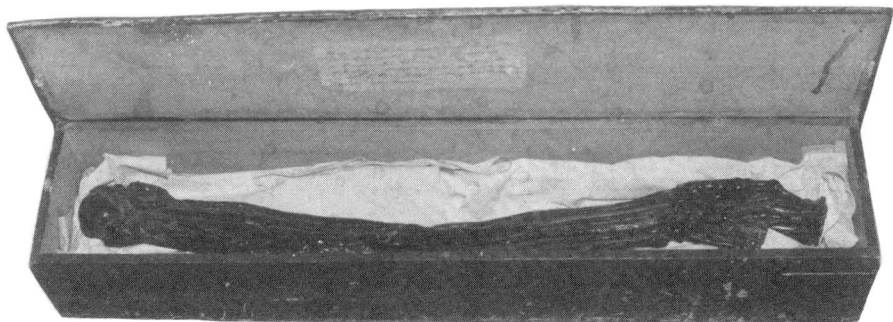

Petrified arm of George Carpenter, hanged in 1813
as found in its original wooden box
(Photo J Girvan)

49

EXECUTION

Illustration from a Broadsheet, Devizes Prison
(Author's Collection)

Piece of Skin

Another piece of body from a hanged man came up for sale when a piece of preserved skin belonging to William Burke was auctioned in Devizes at the local collectors' auction in 1992. This gruesome memento looked like a small piece of leather and was accompanied by a letter of authentication dated 1890.

The 37 year old Irish man was part of the Burke and Hare duo, known as the notorious Victorian body snatchers, who were hanged in Edinburgh in 1829. They had been supplying the medical profession with freshly murdered bodies.

Burke's own body after his execution was donated to the Royal College of Surgeons in Edinburgh where it was dissected and small pieces of skin sold as souvenirs.

WITCHES AND WIZARDS

Witches were not uncommon in the Devizes area during the 16th and 17th Centuries. Certain men and women were thought to have a covenant with the Devil, doing evil work in the parish. They could stir up storms and lightening to damage farmers' crops, cause illness and infant deaths. In 1558 Parliament legislated that witches should be killed and destroyed. By 1563 the Parliament Bill was passed and so a witchhunt began.

An old woman was imprisoned and put to death in Devizes in 1667 after she had been found making a wax image of a person into which she stuck pins, causing death. People were afraid of witches, it was thought if a witch was able to acquire parts from your body such as nail parings, hair cuttings and extracted teeth, they could be used against you. Parents were afraid that children's teeth after falling out could get into the hands of a witch and be used to harm them, and so the story of the Tooth Fairy came about to ensure that children's teeth could be kept safe.

The practise of "pricking" was used in this area when spikes were pricked into the flesh and under fingernails. If the victim could feel no pain this would indicate she was a witch, but characters like the notorious Matthew Hopkins were known to have a pricker with a retractable spike to ensure no pain. A witchfinder was paid handsomely for a successful confession.

In 1652 at the Quarter Sessions William Star was committed as having a "fraternity with an evil spirit". He was stripped and when unusual spots were found on his body, this was considered proof as contact with the devil. Numerous old women were subject to this bizarre searching of skin accompanied by hideous torture to extract a confession.

Witches should be burned or their corpses staked into the ground to prevent them returning as a ghost to haunt. It was thought the duration a witch could fly in the air on a besem broomstick was as long as she could hold her breath. It would therefore take a series of flights to reach her destination.

The following recipe was known to have been used for a witch's broth to assist a Satanic Ritual:-

> *"The liver of a hare, nail parings*
> *entrails of a toad, barley and rags."*

Original Victorian Stereoscopic Slide "The Ghost"
(Author's Collection)

The Devizes Wizard

In 1624 the erratic mischievous exploits of Cantelow, the Devizes Wizard, was attracting public attention. The very strange story is recorded how he was called upon to inflict his wizardry on an event that happened at the village of Wilcot. The Reverend W Palmer refused to permit a stranger visiting the village to ring the church bell. It was an inconsiderate request so late in the evening as Sir George Wroughton's house was so near to the church.

Cantelow agreed to help the man revenge the vicar by causing the church bell to ring continuously of its own accord. This uncanny ceaseless tolling attracted many people, including the Detector General of Imposters to King James I, to come from London to investigate.

The local community had been suffering from this and numerous other mischievous magic antics of Cantelow, consequently he was committed to the county jail at Fisherton, Salisbury for a life sentence during which he vowed that the bell would continue to mysteriously ring during his internment. On the death of the King, Cantelow was liberated from his imprisonment and true to his word, on his release, the bell stopped ringing.

52

Cantelow, The Devizes Wizard (Waylen Print)

The following witch's incantation was written by Benjamin Johnson in the 17th century, from B H Cunnington's research.

*"To make ewes cast their lambs, swine eat their farrow
and housewives turn not work, nor the milk churn,
Writhe children's wrists and suck their breath in sleep.
Get vials of their blood and where the sea cast up slimy
ooze, search for a weed to open locks and rivet charms,
Plant about in the wicked feat of all mischiefs which
are manifold."*

DETECTION

There are many ways to attempt detection of supernatural spirits or souls of the dead commonly referred to as ghosts. As a historian the author does not have experienced knowledge in this specialised subject.

The traditional basic gadgets for detection are dowsing rods, a bobbler and a pendulum which are used as sensitive extensions to the body senses. Functioning as aerials or antennae the dowsing rods are hand held and are directed towards a potential energy source, they swing together or apart to indicate a reaction.

The bobbler is a similar single rod incorporating a coil while pendulum dowsing is often used in conjunction with a map to determine locations.

In this technological age sophisticated electronics have been developed to pick up a wide range of senses. Thermal image cameras are able to photograph hot spots and images, while thermal meters can detect the other end of the thermal scale, cold spots are usually associated with ghost images. A time lapse camera is used to record on film a very slight movement undetectable by the eye. Other metering equipment can be used for night detection using infra-red. Photon sensors for picking up light, magnetometers for magnetism and ultrasonic receivers for picking up sounds on that level. Most objects emit a frequency which can be detected with super low and super high frequencies as in the study of physics.

How you interpret collated data gives rise to considerable debate in the world of science.

There are strange gadgets that appear to operate without a power source such as the copper induction coil which is an emitter, also the copper helical spiral which can be rotated by human energy but without physical contact. The "Ouija Board" is used to make contact with the spirit world and the "Planchette" communicates by writing but it is unadvisable to experiment with these items without experienced knowledge as harm can be caused through ignorance.

THE WALK

Many different groups of people have been on the Ghost Walk which are held during the autumn, winter evenings to take advantage of the dark. Some from as far away as Australia, Canada, Japan, France and America.

It is not an unusual sight to see a group of people gingerly walking along backstreets and alleyways of the town in the shadows of the night in the company of the author. People with varying outlooks all sharing a common curiosity have been on the walk, from family groups, organisations and clubs, to members of a spiritual paranormal society.

The site of the gallows is a very strong area for dowsing when numerous people have picked-up a reaction. A sense of presence seems to radiate at this spot which has witnessed a gruesome past history. Locations on the walk have produced strange inner feelings when sightings have been made, but it must be said that not everyone has an ability to see "things".

However all the young boys in a scout troupe could see a man burying something at the bottom of his garden while on the Ghost Walk one evening. "Just what was he burying?"

The walk was brought to life on the radio one autumn when James Harrison made a recording for BBC Wiltshire Sound to include mysterious background music and sound effects.

Events have happened during these evenings which have caused great excitement when "Lady Isabella" was seen in Castle Lane, and a hooded figure in black was also seen at another location while on the walk.

Ghost Walk at Devizes Market Cross (Photo A Girvan)

Spontaneous
Image
Photographed
at Poulshot
1994
(Author's Collection)

ACKNOWLEDGEMENTS

With grateful thanks to the following:-
Wiltshire Archaeological and Natural History Society
Devizes Museum, Library Resources

Andrew Barnard, Duncan Collins, Olive Chivers, Carol Cross,
Lord Carter, Elizabeth Duck, James Harrison, C J Megraw,
Ralph Pike, Joan Pressley, Les Reeves, Paul Shearing,
Anne Saddington, Bill Underwood, John Watkins, Margaret Worth.
Wiltshire County Police
Christine Aloma Stanbridge (Physic Medium)
Phoenix Spiritual Development Group of Calne,
Thanks to Kate Fenn for her expertise

Particular thanks to Norman Ellis for his photography
Alistair Renvoize for allowing reproduction of his artwork,
including an especially commissioned drawing for the book,
Marilyn Greenwood who typed the manuscript

and finally, all who have been on the Ghost Walk and those
who have contributed other information.

"But have you been on the Ghost Walk?"